Photographic Prayers 2

The Holy Island of Lindisfarne explored through images and words.

by Mary, Mark and Aurian Fleeson

This first edition published by:
Lindisfarne Scriptorium Limited,
Farne House, Marygate,
Holy Island of Lindisfarne,
TD15 2SJ, United Kingdom.
www.lindisfarne-scriptorium.co.uk

ISBN-13: 978 1 909041 26 4

10 9 8 7 6 5 4 3 2 1

British Library Cataloguing in Publication Data - a catalogue record for this book is available
from the British Library.

Typeset by Lindisfarne Scriptorium Limited.
Book production and preparation by Burning Light Solutions Limited.
Printed and bound in the UK.

Dedicated to our parents with love and thanks x

New life
Budding,

New light
Dawning,

New hope
Growing.

The sunlight on those leaves
Will not be the same
As it is today.

The clouds will be different
Behind the branches,
Beyond the trees.

Treasure this precious moment
And the next one,
And the next.

Then at times when there seems
Little to treasure,
Remember.

LOOK AROUND,
REALLY LOOK,
THIS MOMENT,
THIS BREATH,
THIS LIGHT,
THIS LIFE,
WILL
NEVER

BE

THE

SAME.

Daisy yellow,
Daisy white,
Daisy leaves so green.

Such a simple flower,
Yet what a tale to tell.

Yellow for the crown
Of the King,
White for the purity
Of the Lamb,
Green for the promise
Of new life.

Such a simple flower,
Yet what a tale to tell.

The sea spray splashes,
It rises, roughly reaching,
A petite, perfect posy,
Of frothing, fizzing foam.

Let pure love,
Rise unbound in me,
A cleansing, powerful soak,
Of passionate worship.

I'm here again,
Down by the upturned boats.
Dreaming of the things of life,
Wandering by the shore.

I'm here again,
Touching history, hearing time.
Pondering the whys of life,
Imagining the what ifs.

Landlocked anchor,
Resting on the ground,
Holding onto nothing,
Embedded into nothing.

Like the proverbial,
Square peg,
In a round hole,
In the wrong place,
At the wrong time.

A message perhaps?
To all who feel
They don't belong...

Hold onto love,
Hope for rightness,
Embed yourself in truth,
Seek God,
And wherever you are,
Be love.

Sea weathered,
Bleached and shaped,
Seasoned and polished
By storm and sand.

Roughness smoothed,
Sculpted by the Great Artist
And imagined from seed
By the same.

15

If these stones could speak,
What tales would they tell?
Would they hold forth about gentle tides
and fierce winds?
Or whisper stories of human goodness
and common frailty?

If each pebble had a word,
Would they combine in a poem?
An epic saga of ships and toil
and courage unlimited?
A limerick of laughter, a plea of prayer,
a ballad of life?

If every shell had a song,
What tune would prevail?
Would it fill our dreams,
become the soundtrack of life?
A lilting narrative of love and hope
and life everlasting?

They sat - comfortably wrapped in coats and hats,
Protected against the sea-scented winds,
But it still chilled their knees and ankles, cheeks and noses.

Every year - the same bench, same time of year,
Breathing in the sea-scented air,
Watching the ever changing clouds, the sun on the water.

Years passed - time rolled on, gathered souls,
Left the bench waiting in the sea-scented breeze,
Silently observing the ever changing scene.

What meaning can we gather?

A lone guidepost,
Surrounded by an endless sea.
Alone, it leads nowhere,
it just stands,
it just is.

But it is just one of many,
And together,
Together they become a path,
Together they lead somewhere,
Onward, forward, beyond...

What meaning can we gather?

Pilgrim will you pause,
Ponder awhile in this holy place,
    Touch with your soul,
    Gaze with your heart.

Pilgrim will you breathe,
Deeply inhale the Spirit in this place,
    Touch with your soul,
    Gaze with your heart.

Pilgrim will you rest,
Let the breeze carry your worries away,
    Touch with your soul,
    Gaze with your heart.

As the ages pass they expose,
And the outgoing tide reveals,
The core, strong structure that remains.

As the Spirit within grows it exposes,
Like the outgoing tide it reveals,
The bare, naked beauty, that is you.

Fire in the sky,
Glowing horizon,
Memories evoked,
Of times gone by.

Fire from the north,
Warring and taking,
Disturbing peace,
In times gone by.

Fire in the sky,
A new interpretation,
Light bringing hope,
In times to come.

I could sing of this sky forever,
A song of colour and glory,
Vivid shades,
Ever changing.

Would that I could hold this beauty,
(Would that I could hold His Hand,)
And have it transform,
(Have His love transform,)
In a moment,
My heart.

I could sing of His love forever,
A song of passion and hope,
True love,
Never fading.

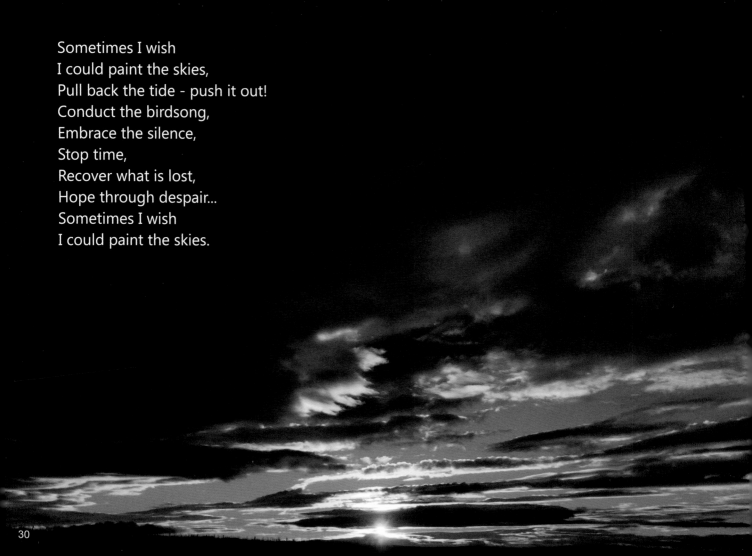

Sometimes I wish
I could paint the skies,
Pull back the tide - push it out!
Conduct the birdsong,
Embrace the silence,
Stop time,
Recover what is lost,
Hope through despair...
Sometimes I wish
I could paint the skies.

For an eternity - merely hours,
Suspended - tortured.
For an eternity - three days,
Descended - separated.
For an eternity- truly forever,
Ascended - reunited.

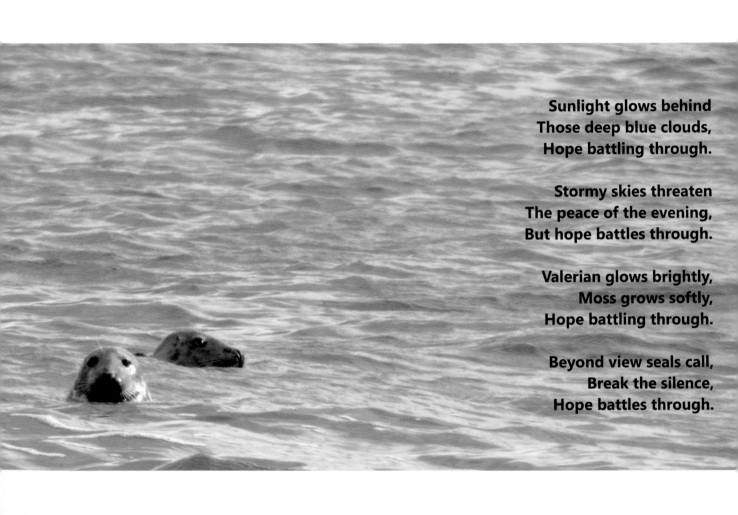

Sunlight glows behind
Those deep blue clouds,
Hope battling through.

Stormy skies threaten
The peace of the evening,
But hope battles through.

Valerian glows brightly,
Moss grows softly,
Hope battling through.

Beyond view seals call,
Break the silence,
Hope battles through.

35

The stillness,
Like time suspended,
Silently screams...
Remember this moment,
This calm, this peace.

Hold it in your heart,
And mind,
Embed it in your soul.

The monochrome tones,
Shadowed silhouettes,
Tell the story of contrasts,
Stark messages, boldly told.

Hold them in your heart,
And mind,
Embed them in your soul.

The stories, ancient as time,
Are yours and mine,
Good and bad,
And all shades between.

Hold them in your heart,
I'll hold them in mine,
With hope, we will
Embed them in our souls.

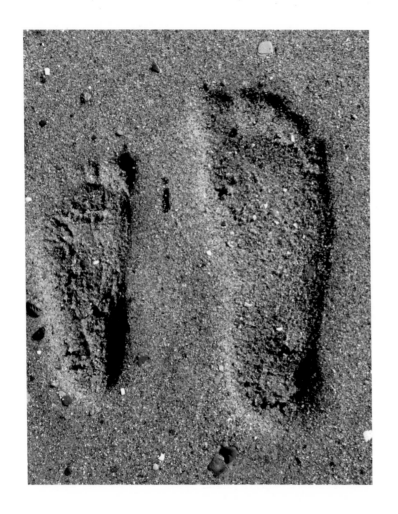

How quickly the years pass,
Feet and hands growing,
Hearts and minds expanding.

Bittersweet the years pass,
Strength and knowledge growing,
Love and understanding expanding.

All our hopes and all our fears,
Rest,
In those feet and hands
Following,
Those hearts and minds
Loving.

In just the right moment the light can transform
Ordinary skies,
Into a promise.

In just the right moment The Light can transform
Ordinary people,
With a promise.

Moments, maybe hours, perhaps a lifetime,
Wondering, pondering, considering,
What lies beyond, hidden from sight?

What lies beyond the dunes?
Sharp grasses, slippery golden sand?
Or azure skies and calm blue seas?

What lies beyond the edge of today?
Endless trials, complex challenges?
Or azure skies and calm blue seas?

Moments, maybe hours, perhaps a lifetime,
Wondering, pondering, considering,
What lies beyond, hidden from sight?

Only going forward will answer.
Only light will defeat the dark,
Only fear will spoil the view.

Dear Friend,

The photographs in this book were all taken by us over the last three years, most were taken with various incarnations of iPhones and digital SLR's.

We hope you have enjoyed them as much as we enjoyed capturing these unique moments in time.

All of the words were written by Mary in response to the images.

Mary, Mark & Aurian, Holy Island, 2017.

Looking from Chare End.

Looking towards Bamburgh.

Spring buds.

Churchyard tree.

Priory through the tree

Wild daisies near Jenny Bell's.

Looking towards St. Cuthbert's Island.

Waves on rocks at Coves Bay.

Detail of Herring Boat hut by the Ouse.

Abandoned anchor.

Driftwood below castle.

By the pier.

Pebbles, shells & fosssils.

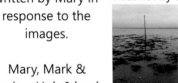

Pilgrim Way from Chare Ends at high tide..

Pilgrim Way from Chare Ends at low tide..

St. Cuthbert's Island.

Remains of old jetty.

Lane to Jenny
Bell's Well.

Looking towards the mainland.

Pilgrim's Way towards mainland.

Looking towards
the mainland.

Detail of Herring Boat
hut by the Ouse.

Looking towards Bamburgh.

Cross from
Hetton Hall chapel*.

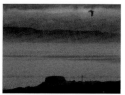
St. Cuthbert's Island.

Seals off Coves Bay.

Bench overlooking
the Ouse

Wild valerian.

The Ouse, one very still morning.

Old jetty post.

Mother & son
footprints.

Looking from Chare Ends.

Rainbow over fields.

Priory through
the trees.

Sand dunes.

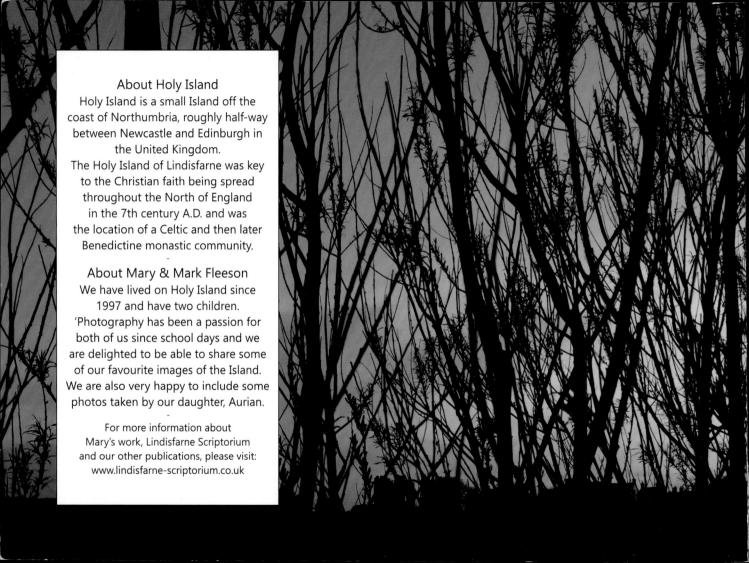

About Holy Island
Holy Island is a small Island off the
coast of Northumbria, roughly half-way
between Newcastle and Edinburgh in
the United Kingdom.
The Holy Island of Lindisfarne was key
to the Christian faith being spread
throughout the North of England
in the 7th century A.D. and was
the location of a Celtic and then later
Benedictine monastic community.

-

About Mary & Mark Fleeson
We have lived on Holy Island since
1997 and have two children.
'Photography has been a passion for
both of us since school days and we
are delighted to be able to share some
of our favourite images of the Island.
We are also very happy to include some
photos taken by our daughter, Aurian.

-

For more information about
Mary's work, Lindisfarne Scriptorium
and our other publications, please visit:
www.lindisfarne-scriptorium.co.uk